G000057116

Augustus Rains has an inte
of writers who appear to have knowledge
beyond that of the ordinary working person.

He looked at religious text and found a
questioning, inquiring mind.

His belief is that of a universal intelligence
surrounding our home planet and every sentient
being is a part of it.

It is to this that we return.

To my wife Rose, thank you for your
kindness and compassion in the
nature of love

Augustus Rains

Verse

of

A

Free

Thinker

Copyright Augustus Rains 2023

The right of Augustus Rains to be identified as author of this work has been asserted by the author in accordance with sections 77 and 78 of the Copyright, Designs and Patents Act 1988.

All rights reserved. No part of this publication may be reproduced, stored in a retrieval system, or transmitted in any form or by any means, electronic, mechanical, photocopying, recording, or otherwise, without the prior permission of the publishers.

Any person who commits any unauthorised act in relation to this publication may be liable to criminal prosecution and civil claims for damages.

A CIP catalogue record for this title is available
from the British Library.

ISBN 9798385539376

Published by Amazon

Foreword

This book is of poems created on the authors everyday thinking about everyday experiences in this everyday life. Analytical thinking is the key, in the authors veiw, to knowing and attempting to understand the complex problems of this, the human condition in which we find ourselves.

In this 70 to 80 years of this average life span many attempts are made to better oneself and the key, in the authors veiw, to doing this is by considering others in an unselfish way and promoting kindness and goodness to everyone.

In this respect I believe that we can indeed reap as we have sown.

Contents   page

Comment by the author ~

Personal Responsibility I believe
is part of our Duty of Care to
everybody else as well as to
ourselves

To my Mother, I Ask

My Mum, your happiness I see anew
Now, here in my life at this early stage
I would like very much to know from you
How a person should become wise of age

How to be so loved and how to love life
To know and to love the earth's nature song
And how in living to battle with strife
So then to keeping me freely from wrong

How to know on earth mankind's destiny
For what will the world be showing to me?
The face of this planet's adversity
Or some adventure my future to be

Dear Mother of mine, be true to your task
In your loving and motherly action
Can it not be too much for me to ask?
That you be such likeness to perfection

Comment by the author ~

The first poem is a person looking down from heaven ready to incarnate in a life on this earthly plane. The parents chosen and the life to lead would, in the long run, be to learn and experience life lessons needed to advance spiritually.

This advancement would be fully realised back in heaven.

The following poem is the chosen Mother's reply to her child which shows her full understanding of the situation. The Mother must do the best for her child as she too is on a spiritual path.

To My Child I Reply

Dearest Child, I love you beyond every
measure
I have gazed upon you in my most happy
dreams
You are indeed I know, a most precious
treasure
Much more than I could ever imagine, it
seems

Beautiful child of this vast cosmic
universe
Here in this warring age of
civilisations
Gladly you came to me your nature I now
nurse
Amid mankind's constant, tribal,
confrontations

Have faith your gracious stay on earth be truly
grand
With fellow travellers who, on this earthly
plane
Have the love and wisdom of a devoted
band
With some enlightened expression to so
explain

And when the mysteries of life for you
unfold
Gaze through the dawning of creation's
mistiness
Take courage, be truthful, be wise, be very
bold
Then may you dare to walk in divine
happiness

Comment by the author ~

The following poem "Our Planet"
was inspired by my parental thoughts of
preserving the earth for generations to come.

Bearing in mind that in reincarnation, the sins of
the fathers (from the Christian Bible) would be
visited on ourselves reincarnating two or three
generations down the line. Thus, we would reap
as we have sown. Far better, I think, to sow
earthly goodness and love to all sentient beings.

Our Planet

In this life-giving sunlit ball
When its light went away to night
It full-circled round, then did call
To see the dawning of morning light

I gazed at nature bye and byes
Its warm light air to truly sense
On earth with my clear-seeing eyes
In such bewildering pleasance

I saw earth give of its beauty
For myself its life is so strong
To care for it, is my duty
Lest I myself do it some wrong

I will then suffer its action
For its action will surely come
If, in my careless destruction
My greed cannot be overcome

Comment by the author ~

Our planet Earth can sustain all life forms in abundance with everything that civilizations and nature needs to survive.

But, it cannot sustain greedy people

Peoples of the World

Peoples of the graceful white dove
Unite and then together fight
In harmony for peace and love
Make war and conflict take to flight

And so banish all ill-feeling
From nations of the world to nations
With talk of good-will prevailing
Reach out, give congratulations

And joy of living be for all
The right to life being honoured
Compassion felt for all who fall
To help their precious lives savoured

So to dreaming is not in vain
For it must one day come to pass
All who sow love is all who gain
In a world pure with pleasantness

In the following poem are yet again thoughts of
nature, how wonderful it is ~

Tree and Flower

With root and branch and born to live
Grow in fullness strong and firm
Your peace and love stretch out to give
In heat of day and rage of storm

Tree of beauty with swaying leaves
Blossoms young in newness of spring
By lake and sky and blowing waves
Sun, wind and rain conspire to bring

Each year as winter season fades
And nature wakes in warmth of day
The springtime with flower cascades
Adorning earth's garlanded way

And the summer heightens on high
Where seas of grass on windswept flow
Birds on trees fly on pale blue sky
Over meadow where wild flower grow

The Seasons

Wind and snow of winter surge
Fading glory of green meadow
With forest, mountain, lake and herb
And blooms of greying cloud billow

The spring in its newness of life
With fresh buds climbing to sunlight
What a struggle for them, such strife
To bathe in brilliance bright

Summer blossoms, colours brightness
Breeze and warm sun down on my back
A feeling of warmth and lightness
Enters life and I stay on track

Then the gold of summer passing
With sunlight low in pale blue sky
Soft cooling breeze and leaves falling
Make ready for autumn nearby

Winter Festivities

Loving Christmas, jingle bell chimes
And having passed the shortest day
New hopes and dreams of coming times
The fresh New Year is on its way

Amid the frosty wind and snow
Stars that glitter on clear still night
Rejoicing by a firelight glow
With bountiful gifts to delight

Cheerful parties and young romance
Such splendour on those chance meetings
Mingled with the magic of dance
And banqueting with new greetings

Singing happy songs by the score
Hearty friends, good talk, jolly cheer
Feasting and finest wines galore
To celebrate the coming year

Hibernation

Slowing with the cold coming on
And autumn mild turning to chill
Warm summer long faded and gone
Gathers the frost on plain and hill

Furry creatures go to and fro
Making for to sleep from drowsy
Land becoming covered in snow
Bury burrows warm and cosy

Weather reaching the earth turning
And the sun its rays lying low
Touching the world on its edging
On horizon cast just a glow

On hardest ground the life is still
In frozen cold, gale of winter
Sleeping on through the seasons chill
Awakening not from slumber

Horizons

The night comes in as sunlight fades
And scattered hues of coloured ray
Dance on fair-weather cloud cascades
Farewell the sun at end of day

And a still silence of night air
Brings heavenly star scattered light
Open sky, new horizons clear
Bringing distant hopes to delight

A new day the dawn appearing
And a new light from rising sun
A new course the helm now steering
And a new venture to be done

Set the good sails on fairest breeze
To plough the bow through ocean blue
And with true sailors mind at ease
Take the waves of life through and through

The following poem from childhood wishes
grows to adult thinking ~

Wishes

I wish… and I wish… for I wish
Chocolates, sweets and things to eats
But again for what can I wish
Ice creams, chips and all goody treats

Brightly coloured birthday cakies
And fabulous party galores
Colourful Halloween dresses
And Christmas things with Santa Clause

Candles glowing to blowing out
Wishing to wish upon a dream
Aladdin's lamp, genies about
Arabian nights, stars that gleam

Galloping knights in armour bright
Sporting shields and swords and lances
And pirate ships ready to fight
Seas, islands, fanciful places

Sailing a wave upon its crest
Under starry constellations
To a haven of perfect rest
To wish in my imaginations

See light of an evening sunset
To night-times world of stars give way
And in its turn comes dawn to let
A brightness of a brand new day

On this globe circling round the sun
And to wish upon life's treasures
For happiness of so much fun
And for more of earthlings pleasures

Wishing freedom to overcome
With things to think and to have thought
And to see things already done
Adversities already fought

Comment by the author ~

In the following poem,
'Life on the Edge'

I have tried to show simple but very
beautiful things on this earth that our
wonderful planet mostly gives in
abundance.

Things that, as it would appear will
only be appreciated by some of
mankind when they are destroyed
and gone.

Life on the Edge

A diamond from a darkened place
A pebble from a sunlit beach
A thousand islands, a blue space
A mountain high to sky doth reach

And ocean depths in deepest blue
With creatures moving up and down
And coral reefs in shallows to
So fragile do they wear their crown

For mankind on this earth cares not
The plight of corals delicate
So why the seas he then forgot?
Engaged in quarrels intricate

And climate change doth take on pace
Disaster ever coming near
Perhaps the earth might show some grace?
To me down here it's not so clear

Comment by the author ~

In the following poem,
'Find a Purpose in Life'

Some waste their lives with
unnecessary indulgencies
and watch others suffer.

Whilst their riches grow,
they do nothing

Find a Purpose in Life

May your souls rise on eagle wing
May you see your true worthiness
May your grace so to loved ones sing
May you gain heights of happiness

We are of origin unknown
Perhaps not of our own making
But where seeds of life have been sown
We see cycles of creating

But then what of a purpose in life?
Does it all come so to nothing?
This world's merry-go-round circus
Do we then cease in existing?

But I would rather not think so
We must carry on, go forward
In unknown ventures, our minds glow
To seek and to know, go onward

But when they return and suffer
hardships themselves, what then?

Reincarnation

Your past lives now come before you
And with all your moan and your groan
Your habits with this life anew
You take on all you have past sown

Take without any dread nor fear
Despair never coming so near
Now carrying on year on year
So a new path to ever steer

With fortitude forgive the past
All your foes of mind now a-cast
Your future in goodness shall last
At your repentance now aghast

Then be glad what happens occurs
And so work out your karmic life
Your very life giving soul stirs
Amongst all your soul living strife

The following is an extract from my book,
'A Tale of Crystal Visions'

The scene is a cavern below a castle where the
Witch lays hold of a rock of crystal.

The Crystal reflects her true self.

THE WITCH SORINDA

"Where lay the magic of the world?
The bowel of earth I do expect,
where? The wealth I desire to hold,
where? In my mind I do detect

"But what of the treasures I sought
in all these long years of cunning?
Brrr! Me thinks a shiver I caught.
Huh! Me thinks tears come a-running

"The crystal does reflect my mind
my past behaviour magnified.
But look there, was I so unkind?
Ah! Those childhood virtues that died

"Those shapes appearing I see clear
my early years of happiness,
loved ones I held so very dear
later years turning to sadness

"When Lucifer came on the scene,
and then melted rhyme and reason,
I see my youth being quite clean
he with me did commit treason.

"And took from me a noble life
giving instead a cross to bear
heavily with trouble and strife
my life does now asunder tear."

(End of extract)

Looking to the Future

I seek a goal so elusive
I go and so forth to venture
It can be nothing conclusive
I find it to be mere conjecture

So disappointment ensnares me
I keep looking for reasons why
I gaze up at God-like to see
With pointed finger to the sky

Thinking, what is it to my score?
Why then be this imposition?
I can't receive what I ask for
So captive my mind's delusion

Better cast off the fading past
And move on, let go of grasping
It's history, things never last
Progress, to the future casting

Passing Time

To look for doing is my task
Which includes the whole human race
What more is there to go and grasp
Than to behold my life in grace

But many do chase useless gift
Many treasures unlimited
Many minds from place to place shift
Taking things contaminated

With greed take objects of desire
And look to things for fulfilment
With each other they do conspire
To find in pursuits, contentment

But in the end is much despair
It never happens as they think
They then to others do compare
And their moods change near to the brink

Comment by the author ~

The previous poem, 'Passing Time'
refers to a purpose being in my life.
Is the purpose positive or negative?
Is the outcome one of happiness?

Or is it, as I reach out to my limits
of disappointment that I fall back
from the brink of despair?
If I don't, then an unthinkable
end awaits me.

The following poem,
'Where has all the Time Gone?'
makes me think of not wasting time
nowadays so much in idle pursuits.

To look for a positive purpose like
developing compassion for all living
beings can bring happiness for all
peoples in all of nature.

Where has all the Time Gone?

Then did pass bye my younger days
To now, an elderly person
With memories of childhood ways
Where has all the passing time gone?

Many years of happy marriage
Since we first together began
We then rode in horse and carriage
Where has all the passing time gone?

Children born, children grow and cry
They make children, some more than one
With so much our history gone bye
Where has all the passing time gone?

How others, they think the same thing
They asked as their mind's thinking shone
With questions, questions their minds bring
Where has all the passing time gone?

The following poem is here
because at times in my life
I have suffered from one thing
or another as many have, so
I thought that if we loved
everyone we would not want
to destroy anybody.
Instead we would look after
everyone and care for their
health and nourishment.

There would be,
No Wars.
No Famine.
No Pestilence.

Taken from my book 'A Tale of
Crystal Visions'
The scene is in a cavern below a castle
where a Mystic Gnome is talking
to a repentant Witch Sorinda

Suffering

"If you suffered not as you have,
shallow would be the depth of you
void of humility and love
your very self not really true

"If you suffered not as you have,
shallow the compassion in you
void of feeling kindness and love
your very self not really true

"If you suffered not as you have,
shallow the sensing within you
void of deep emotion and love
your very self not really true

"If you suffered not as you have,
shallow nature's wisdom in you
void of insight thinking and love
your very self not really true."

The following poem is again
taken from my book,
"A Tale of Crystal Visions"

It is better thought of in the
context of eternal life within
this, our brief, passing incarnation.

I believe that we have differing
incarnations and in them we
experience all the things in the poem.

I believe that we have to live experiences
and go through everything to make us better,
more understanding people.

So rich or poor in the long run
matters not for we all, hopefully
reach our destination ~ heaven

It Matters Not

It matters not what garb you wear
Or from where or why you should come
Or if you should dark or fair
It matters not in the long run

It matters not your wealth nor fame
Or your total monetary sum
Or your power or famous name
It matters not in the long run

It matters not if great or small
Or of talents done or not done
Or if you should be short or tall
It matters not in the long run

It matters not, sad or joyful
If happiness stays or is gone
Or if you're glad or sorrowful
It matters not in the long run

It matters not who come and go
Or in darkness or in the sun
Or if you should be fast or slow
It matters not in the long run

It matters not your life be torn
Or salvation a distant sun
Or if survival seems forlorn
It matters not in the long run

It matters not the prayers you send
Or all the powers of the hymn
Or the things that come to an end
It matters not in the long run

It matters not how high you climb
For of all these things you consist
Nor the total length of your time
For in all these things you exist

Comment by the author ~

In my developing youth,
my thoughts a true mix of emotions,
in times of turmoil and turbulence
my wonderings about existence
rife with unrest.

To find a loved one I believe is
a tremendous gift in life.

The following poem is a story
of love found and of the living
together thereafter helping
each other through adversity.

To a Loved One

My Dear, as now I look at you
And reflect how I fell in love
I see your face, I gladly knew
Your heart as like a gentle dove

I loved you in fields of green
We there did vow never to part
Young were we and a-courting seen
Happy in love and life to start

We did make our promises too
In those faraway days gone bye
When making memories with you
I sang then and now gladly cry

For past adventures and turmoil
That stays with us both forever
With tide and time marking their toil
What they threw, we took together

The love of togetherness continues ~

I called to One I Loved

In crisis I became tethered
No one step here, no one step there
And my free thoughts I so gathered
Then once up here, so once down there

I won so hard and lost so fast
In my delight I turned aghast
To see such fortunes come by crashed
That they, not for long, did they last

I did stumble and badly stall
And then in despair, I did fall
To one I loved I did so call
And then thereafter I stood tall

For paths I trod had disasters
And as diamonds likened to souls
With good facets cut by Masters
Together did achieve my goals

Comment by the author ~

The previous poem came to me in my
meditations.

After much soul searching
on spiritual matters in the
presence of like-minded people
came the verse,

'Our souls are like diamonds
With facets cut by Masters'

This with other poems were
self-published and printed
under a pen-name,
'Moston Circle'

The copyright was given to
Moston Spiritualist Church
Manchester, England

The love of togetherness continues ~

Our Love Story

On our voyage we truly say
With this we can be nothing less
Than love forever and a day
To travel on in time endless

For into void we have no fear
And side by side is joy indeed
At times in life we cast a tear
Loves true belief, our very creed

Our own true love we do caress
In many days of happiness
Without each other life is less
Not going on in happiness

For gracious love is like a dream
Heaven, a dream of paradise,
You be that portrait of a dream
You make this world a paradise

And we find that ~

We Are Capable

We expect the unexpected
And we think the unthinkable
And each time we stay connected
Life becomes more incredible

We do undoable doing
And we find the unfindable
And each time in mindful thinking
We reach, grasp the unreachable

We stand amazed at new meaning
At new-found realisations
At new-found paths we are treading
And always there are new questions

We then learn the unlearnable
Question the unquestionable
We achieve the unachievable
And find that, 'we are capable'

Comment by the author ~

I think that we are indeed capable of
overcoming the world's injustices,
of making a better life for everyone,
everyone without exception.

All we need to do is to believe in ourselves
and realise a new world of
true compassion and kindness
which are themselves in the nature of love.

The following poem is rather like seeing
through a delusion. Delusions occur all the
time but we cannot be fooled forever.
To be fooled forever is a terrifying thought.

We must see the folly of conflict and greed,
of conniving, conceit and treachery.

When we find that inner peace is there for
us and when we see it through all the outside
interferences, we can then control our
lives and our living more responsibly.

See Beyond Our Lives

See through dogmatic ritual
And not be bound by what we find
Those nonsense things and fictional
Oh! That elusive peace of mind

We're bombarded by media
Making our thoughts such as some think
Subject to some criteria
We follow and blink and they blink

We're controlled by clever people
Searching ways of making money
It's like climbing a high steeple
From below it's rather shaky

For such a system cannot last
The ways our lives and works advance
When we, the situations grasp
They, then to us cease to entrance

A Cross To Bear

Some defects in the human form
Cause people much trouble and strife
It would appear to be the norm
That for some, in most of their life

Have so to live with much concern
Their abilities limited
Sometimes their minds cannot discern
To what cause it's attributed

We've all got our crosses to bear
Some groan under a wooden cross
Some able to stand up and care
All through it their cross to caress

Others carry a cross of steel
Some go under, crushed with the weight
Whilst those with courage may see still
Their purpose, be happy their state

Comment by the author ~

The previous poem indicates a burden
that some of us are unable to lighten.

I think that it may apply to most of us
though not all can realise it.

I believe that when difficulties arise
then courage is needed even to
bear a cross of wood.

Even with a cross of steel it is not how
heavy the burden but how it is
assimilated, adapted to and courage
found to be happy with our given lot.

Trials and burdens in this earthly life
I believe are to make us stronger for a
greater purpose yet to come on the
higher side of life ~ heaven

Comment by the author ~

The following poem refers to the
inevitable which can be looked at
in two ways, the scary way or the
true happier way.

The former comes with the
ignorance of not knowing and
the latter with a happy acceptance
togetherwith the wisdom of
realisation.

Our loved ones are not gone forever.
They are back home in the real
eternal world of spirit which is far
finer than this gross material
world.

Going on Our Way

The Lord of death's itchy
fingers
Groping around our very
souls
We cling on and our life
lingers
As the Grim Reaper claws at his
goals

Drastic about what is to
come?
Does not have to be a
nightmare
Look to people, observe how
some
Do what they do, see how they
care

And we have to go at some
time
So live life in hope to the
full
No time is ever the right
time
We have to, whatever our
will

And reach heaven, truly it's
there
All our loved ones we thought were
gone
Those who, through all our lives still
care
Will greet us in and say,

"Well Done"

Thwarted Expectations

Without others, I am nothing
I can't exist without others
I must cherish life and being
Others happiness so matters

Then to all gods and goddesses
Why cast delusion in my way
You do give forth false promises
From my true path I then do stray

Compassion and kindness is love
Do not give division and lie
Your message should be one of love
And for truth people so do cry

To understand understandings
Realise realisations
To give freedom from sufferings
And fulfil my expectations

The Traveller

Bon Voyage dearest traveller
Endless wanderings to and fro
In the world, such a reveller
Your own flighty get up and go

Living every precious moment
And for as long as it may last
Sunrise to sunset enjoyment
Now, daylight's end, long shadows cast

Then in dreaming your thinking take
To those places, dreams rise to flight
And climb on high for goings sake
In visions with sights to delight

Be alive for another day
From your worldly path not to stray
But, when you return awhile, stay
Reflect with us your time away

Living a Life of Luxury ?

To be rich or then to be poor?
Some of us be most fortunate?
And at the end, what be the score?
Compared to those unfortunate?

Do we gain excess in heaven?
Because of excess down on earth?
Or that for which we have striven?
Do we give away, after birth?

Was fortune destined just for us?
And for others trouble and strife?
Is it comparing what one does?
Were the poor just to be in life?

That way for their just punishment?
For ill deeds so done in their past?
Did they not make their commitment?
To become better people at last?

Comment by the author ~

In the previous poem "Karma,
the law of cause and effect" (Hindu & Buddhist)
is questioned together with the verses,
"To reap as we sow." (Christian Bible) and
"Every action has a reaction" (Issac Newton)

Question after question is posed
to try and understand effects in one's own
life but alas, I just don't know.

Endemic Corruption

It is the system with persons
Some liars more, some liars less
It is persons pushing sermons
Hypocrites, they do not confess

To others secret deeds of greed
They care not in desperate times
For others very much in need
Who come dispossessed from the past

The greedy do not see their ways
Good people have happiness
Without greed happiness then stays
The corrupt live long with sadness

When truth of actions come to light
Greedy minds lay bare and open
Suffer they must their sorry plight
As reaping what they've sown happen

Comment by the author ~

Corruption in many places,
in Government, in Business,
in Criminal Activities.

Some eminent people, feathering
their own pockets to judgement
really must come.

In the following poem human
capacity for compassion appears
to be very scarce towards many
life-forms as we can see throughout
the world.

On this, our home planet, many other
sentient, living beings have consciousness
and can feel suffering.
This is the way of the world but we do not
have to make it worse for them unnecessarily.

Plight of Animals

Once a free fish, put in a bowl
And in circles so does it go
Humans watch with uncaring soul
Care not for that inflicted so

Once a free bird, put in a cage
From perch to perch so does it fly
Human cruelty at high stage
Shown in captive taken from sky

Once a free rabbit, put in a hutch
In such a cramped, restricted place
Where it can hardly move not stretch
Human behaviour, such disgrace!

Once wild and free, put in a zoo
Captive, locked behind bars
Slumped, dejected. What can I do?
Let them roam free under the stars

Question ~ We have the power,
but the wisdom to use it? I fear not.

Comment by the author ~

The thinking on the following poem ~

Our basic needs, food, clothing and shelter which, in an ideal world, everyone should have. To pursue excesses is the human ego and if this can be controlled on one item of desire another will take its place if allowed to do so.

No attachment to things means to say that our ego can't replace one thing with something else if our minds do not allow it.

Being free of the world's material desires to possessing things can lead to our minds being free.

It may not be as easy as one may think but nevertheless, it may be worth a try.

Things

To evolve in my consciousness
Let go of the things that to me cling
The concept, 'to own' meaningless
At end times, nothing does it bring

When the external falls away
Things do not matter anymore
Why cling on as things do not stay?
My consciousness does, I am sure

Come my way, ever more secure
No thoughts of things nor sense of self
As 'things' then become more obscure
For in my mind is now true wealth

I need not have things to possess
Useless trivia I strived for
Conflict and greed that caused distress
Gone! Whatever was it I saw?

Comment by the author ~

In the previous poem 'Things'
refer to material possessions
which I cannot take with me
when I leave this life and go
on my greatest adventure ever.

More Corruption

Do then the corrupt even learn?
And from past mistakes their crowing?
To then so form a new concern?
Of how to alter their doing?

Some do, thank goodness, many don't
They carry on as usual
And don't give a damn the result
But carry on, so casual

Their concepts being blurred indeed
Their careless attitude obscured
To be corrupt, their very creed
Is it endemic? So absurd!

That they see not the light of day
Are blinded by their evil deeds
And carry on in the same way
To their suffering in life's needs

Britannia

Their spirit, strong and glorious
People in this great land of ours
Virtue in deeds victorious
Standing for good in future hours

Of confrontation for justice
In true honourable estate
And in grandeur illustrious
Speak in democratic debate

Enhancing lives in truth sincere
Progress in minds of right thinking
Make compassion, love, our career
Fear not for fear of so shrinking

From our task, do not wayward steer
Keep straight on in truth for the good
Of fellow people we hold dear
Through time their good values have stood

From past adventures to future
War and peace and no surrender
Our heroic deeds to nurture
We face the world our contender

By which we mark our progression
In this world the earth doth to us
And give to us much transgression
From such mundane to glorious

Deeds of great stature and of wealth
Pushing borders of invention
With strong minds and by truest stealth
Make the world our own creation

For the betterment of people
And of creatures both great and small
For in life climbing this steeple
May all be happy standing tall

Comment by the author ~

Perfect Justice, I believe plays itself out
over many lifetimes. In the whole of
creation I believe that this is one of those
open secrets. It's there, one just has to see it.

The following poem, "Rethink our Living"
is advocating a revolution in peaceful
thinking, analysing and with much
reasoning wisdom knowing that compassion
and caring is in the nature of love

Rethink our Living

The world, being run on money
Does give our standing in this life
Our lives being run on money
As without is, nothing but strife

With it our lives are everything
Free to acquire what the world has
Without it, nothing but suffering
Less survive as our lives pass

The rich take a terrible toll
From the work of a working-man
For the rich, more money their goal
The poor survive as best they can

'Tis all grossly inadequate
The unfairness must then be changed
The greedy state is delinquate
And so all must stand rearranged

The Shopaholic

I must have it, I want it now
I need it now so don't delay
To the shop window I then bow
To think to have it lest I stray

From my path of acquiring things
I so delight in what I want
I get it and happiness brings
All the day long I sing and chant

Of things I want to shop for next
To clutter the rooms of my home
More, more lovely things I gets
'Till in home, space no more to roam

But it stops me not on my quest
For it's off again I must go
To look through windows with such zest
And buy, buy, buy that what's on show

Comment by the author ~

The following poem,
'Permission to Think Freely'
was brought about in my thoughts
by questioning just how much people
are influenced by the madia, beliefs,
traditions, established norms and
following the crowd as it were.

It's easy to go along with everybody
else rather than to think independently.
To think for oneself and decide what one
thinks is right and wise.

This, with the knowledge and wisdom
individuals have in the present stage of
development suggests to me that I should
think freely without having to consider so
much that others may agree or disagree.

Permission to Think Freely

You may think that our thoughts are ours
And from influences be free
But do they ask of us favours
Or fall as apples off a tree

Are they guided by force unknown?
Controlled in some mystical way
And to the given reasons shown
Are they true as to what they say?

We can speculate forever
And be none the wiser ever
And the answers we seek, never
Come our way, however clever

As the thinking mind gets confused
And do our thoughts get understood?
As our minds meld together, fused
In free thinking, be that they should

As Our Own

They who overcome tempting thought
Overcome the way of the world
Can win outright a battle fought
But mind lest the paths become blurred

And go out of all proportion
Chasing vanishing illusions
We can get stuck in religion
And take evermore delusions

So rise above the mental strife
Without our getting stuck in sin
Look for purpose and fulfil life
The way of truth and love will win

Searching ourselves within our own
Life, living alongside our own
Understand worlds beyond our own
Have the right to life as our own

The Ending

The world is full of opposites
Where there's good, there is also bad
There's single, also composites
Our thinking, happy also sad

There's being born, also dying
As coming to earth and going
There's catching then also throwing
And doing, so there's not doing

We have belief and unbelief
And we can rot in our own scorn
Or we can turn a fresh new leaf
But think, when from this we are torn

The God concept, a delusion?
Can one prove that it is not so?
Better come to some conclusion
Now, before one departs to go

Comment by the author ~

On the previous poem once more
a question ~

Since mankind formed reasoning ability
there have been many different God concepts
or ideas put into numerous belief systems.

Every concept is different or differing in
some way, therefore I ask ~
"Is it all a delusion"?

The following poem is about some of the
rich, privileged people and their heirs who
rule in greed and selfishness over the poor,
less fortunate in life where some of the
dispossessed are just struggling for mere
existence.

Rulers Come and Rulers Go

The Emperor, on deathbed lay
His subjects pass, bowing, weeping
The Holy Scribes who write and pray
Stand by, dutifully wailing

For, to when the Emperor goes
As in good time he surely will
Those who, in their powerful robes
Unknown their fate, tremble still

In fear of the mindful younger
This new despot will take his place
On a throne he would make stronger
Those who oppose, he would disgrace

He has power of life and death
Life to terminate on a whim
With a frame of mind used in stealth
For lackeys, draped in black, it's grim

Blaming Others

When things don't go right as they should
Some look at a cause, not themself
They blame anything if they could
As it should affect their own wealth

They stand and become very strong
Protecting their own privilege
Not admitting they could be wrong
That to them would be sacrilege

Some do stand and fight, scream and shout
So obstinate be their nature
They twist their faces, look about
Point to others of less stature

Blaming others for their letdown?
NO! This is so grossly unfair
It be themselves, their very own
Shadow of guilt, they lay so bare

From the Past

In the lands of my ancestors
Where warlords fought and many died
Men made subject to conquerors
And the young were killed and they cried

All in the cause of selfish greed
In the few with wealth and power
Who sourced out their own selfish need
They found their dying life sour

For their gains in wealth they took not
To heaven, a greater living
They did not reach, but they did rot
In hells of fire, their own making

Repentance they may swear at times
Seeing the error of their ways
They yearn for to reach better climes
For 'till they do, suffering stays

Beyond Our Home Planet

There is a world beyond our own
So far away in time and space
Where mankind's seed shall soon be sown
In love and peace, to grow in grace

But be careful lest we plunder
As we do our own home planet
Folly we need cast asunder
So not do to new worlds that act

For forgiveness shall not so come
For how much our begging hast grown
In days of old the deeds we've done
We reap the same as that we've sown

Then go explore in love and peace
Good fortune you can then assure
Will come your way and never cease
To gain compassion more and more

Tinkling with God

Is there such a thing as a God?
Or is that a delusion too?
With all life on this earthen sod
Can it be known by just a few?

And what of secrets yet to find?
With reasoning of humankind
Indulging in thoughts of our mind
Can we find a waypost so signed?

Can we know of a secret quest?
And our reaching thoughts satisfied?
That we may have a clue at last?
Our enquiring minds, gratified?

But what is this yet unknown path?
And what is this kind of thinking?
And will it lead to someone's wrath?
And with what are we so tinkling?

Tinkling with Sense

So then where is freedom of thought?
If some confront our questioning
In some belief they be so caught
Do we share that same worshiping?

Or do we think it be fruitless?
Are we to their thinking so caught?
In things that would appear causeless
And then to continue such thought

To be gradually drawing
To belief of some senseless kind
We may cease our mind of thinking?
And salvation, will we, it find?

But this is not human nature
To give in to such things obscure
On some senseless faith adventure
We need to known we are secure

Comment by the author ~

In the following poem the world
refers to societies, cultures and
peoples on the planet earth
whereas the earth refers to the planet
itself whirling through space.

The reference to illusion means
of the world and the ways its
inhabitants think and behave.

Is There a Cure?

This world, is this an illusion?
I haven't got the faintest clue
Perhaps it is mind delusion?
I don't know as to what to do

To find out more about this puzzle
Perhaps my dreams are the real world
Delusion may pour out drizzle
And my very thoughts come out curled

To be true, in my way this gate
So if delusion be not true?
And am I really thinking straight
Or just being without a clue?

At least I know some thoughts are dreams
But in this real life, am I sure?
It is not as clear as it seems
For this thinking, is there a cure?

What's It All About?

It's all about making perfect
In all that I think, say and do
But for some with minds of concrete
Chances of this are very few

So then, wake up you useless band
You drunken clout, lay-about-lout
Leave off a life of vagabond
So standing up, firm, straight and stout

And think of a new thoughtful life
Where consciousness is higher still
Than that so far endured in strife
And the old ways of living, kill

Grab the future with a strong hand
Never let go of that so reached
Goal, laden with treasures so grand
Enter through the veil so far breached

What If?

What if? What if this does happen?
What if? What if that does happen?
What if such a thing does happen?
What if nothing then does happen?

So many concerns and worries
At the prospect of happenings
Dropping on us like snow flurries
Leaving us cold with shiverings

We cannot see or ever know
How they be, so good or so bad
How these things that to us will show
Grief or happiness, glad or sad

But maybe good outcomes for some
May cause many to laugh and feast
And taking them as they may come
Enjoyment for a time at least

Comment by the author ~

In the previous poem,
'What If' show that we can
cause ourselves anxiety by worrying
about what if, but if we said,
"What if we let ourselves live for the
moment and be happy." What then?

In the following poem, 'things'
refer to material possessions which
I cannot take with me when I go
on my greatest adventure ever.

Consciousness

To evolve in my consciousness
Let me let go of my ego
The concept 'to own' meaningless
At end times I have to let go

When the external falls away
'Things' do not matter anymore
Why cling on as 'things' do not stay?
As conscious awareness for sure

Comes my way, ever more secure
No thoughts of 'things' nor sense of self
As 'things' then become more obscure
For in my mind is a true wealth

Awareness is fully forming
Quickening alertness, sensing
Awakening from slumbering
In newness, my life caressing

The Journey's End

We are magic our very self
Our way of life is in giving
Life is found in our very self
Happiness is found in living

Compassion and kindness is love
Joy, happiness, enlightenment
As bright as the flight of a dove
Exhilarating excitement

As now by a soft candle light
Love gathers, held in dreamy skies
Your eyes into mine sparkling bright
In our love-dreams angelic cries

Let us now to this life retire
And then return from whence we came
To a newness of life aspire
To future happiness the same

Comment by the author ~

In the inspirations from meditating
I thought of themes to write about.
Everybody can imagine in this way.
The greatest task is to put all the thinking
into rhyming verse that makes some kind
of sense.

The earth, nature, living is varied and
wondrous. It is really beyond word
description. The more I wonder at it,
the more I find difficulty writing about it.

Therefore, I just now want to be silent
and enjoy the earth's wonderful sense
of creation.

To contemplate in silence like fully realised
spiritual masters and to gain their heights of
wisdom. Is this possible? I may ask but I
won't know unless I try.

An Afterthought

In time, we go onto our way
Pathways to us as yet unknown
We have come so far in our day
Has our togetherness outgrown?

We two together through the storm
And I shall always think of you
Ventures new we go to perform
Your kind are rare and far too few

But to our futures we must go
On this world we take in our stride
Our destiny we do not know
If it will be a gentle ride

We may meet in a future life
On this planet or some other
But still within our conscious strife
We may indeed, be together

Printed in Great Britain
by Amazon

23433565R00057